THE INDOOR GRILL COOKBOOK

EASY AND TASTY GRILLING RECIPES

MARINADES & SAUCES

ROUMIANKA LAZAROVA

Family Approved Recipes

The Indoor Grill Cookbook

Easy and Tasty Grilling Recipes. Marinades & Sauces

Liability Disclaimer

The author reserves the right to amend, supplement, or delete parts of the book or the entire book without special notification or to stop the publication temporarily or finally.

The author disclaims any liability for personal or commercial damages, injuries, losses, errors, omissions resulting from the use, misuse, or misinterpretation of the information provided or contrary interpretation of the subject matter herein. Despite the best-taken efforts, the author does not warrant the accuracy of the information in the book due to rapid changes of information. Any similarities with facts or people are unintentional.

This book is presented solely for informational and motivational purposes only. This book is not intended to provide medical advice of any kind or to replace medical advice, nor to diagnose, prescribe, or treat any illness, disease or injury.

ISBN: 9798675267989
Imprint: Independently published

CONTENTS

R. Lazarova

This page intentionally left blank

INTRODUCTION

With this book, you get 88 fast, delicious, hassle-free recipes for indoor grill on meat, chicken, fish, mushrooms, cheese, and vegetables, marinades, and sauces for them.

My family and friends love to enjoy the so-called indoor grill in all seasons. Whether it is a sunny or rainy day, a warm or cold night, we can prepare our favorite, delicious meals with pleasure, and a mood at home. Indoor grills are versatile and can be easily used by anyone who loves homemade healthy food

Millions of people already use different indoor types of grill options that are cheap to buy: open or covered electric grills, contact grills, grill pans, or cooktop inserts. Why don't you try it? This is another opportunity to enjoy delicious grilled dishes without worrying about using an outdoor grill. Cook safely in your kitchen, on a patio or balcony.

If you already are an indoor grill owner, you'll find ways to perfect your technique and expand your menus with delicious and aromatic ribs, steaks, skewers, meatballs, fish, burgers, cheese, vegetables and mushrooms. With this book, you will get dozens of quick and easy recipes to prepare these delightful surprises. Here you will also find a suitable marinade for your chosen meat, fish, chicken or vegetables. Of course, for your grilled dish to be completed, choose a recipe for a sauce that will complement its taste.

Some subtleties in the roasting

Let us remember some subtleties in the roasting of meat, poultry, fish, cheese, vegetables, and mushrooms on the grill.

- Meat should be *__fresh__* and never frozen.

- Do not buy too lean meats - the grill it will dry further. Buy such a piece of meat on which there is a certain amount of fat in order to make it juicy steak, tenderloin, or chop. *__The fat__* helps the meat to remain tender and juicy even after staying, as it protects the meat juices not to leak and melts into the meat while it is cooking. If you want to reduce the fat, the best approach is to remove them entirely or partly after the meat is already baked instead of before roasting.

- Regarding *__dry (lean) meats__* - wrap the meat in foil or baking paper; inside, add all the spices and must put a piece of butter. If you decide to use baking paper, soak her before placing it on the hot grill, otherwise, it will burn.

- The meat pieces should have **_the same thickness_** for each slice. It is challenging to be cooked evenly meat pieces that have a different thickness.

- Before grilling the meat, it should be **_at room temperature_**.

- Lightly smear the grill surface with vegetable oil or other oil.

- Preheat the grill and place the meat on the grill.

- Grilling time varies depending on the type of meat and **_the thickness of the pieces_** of meat (steaks, chops, fillets, etc.): e.g., 2-3 minutes on each side for steak thickness of 13 mm; 3 - 4 minutes on each side for 25 mm thick steaks; 4 - 6 minutes on each side for steaks with a thickness of 38 - 50mm.

- Place the **_meatballs and sausages_** on the grill and do not press them. Leave them in the form in which you had placed them. This way, they will remain juicy.

- When **_grilling poultry_** must necessarily keep in mind

whether they are whole or sliced. If they are prepared for roasting on a spit, then the cooking time shall be longer and at low heat. If you roast parts of the bird on the grill is better to apply the rules for roasting of meat. In no case should not let the meat burn and turn black.

- The ***fish*** must have fat on itself in order not to stick on the grill. Bake for a short time. If the fish is whole and thick - roast at least 5 minutes on each side. If roast fish fillet with skin, place the fillets skin side down. Bake until it turns white, at least 3-4 minutes on one side only. Do not reverse the tenderloin.

- For ***the cheese*** on the grill commonly are used packages. In such bags, the cheese is warmed very quickly.

- ***The vegetables*** also shall be flavored before being roasted. There are different types of marinades that you can use. Baking time depends on whether the vegetables are whole or cut into pieces. The vegetables are baked quickly.

- When ***mushrooms*** are roasted, it is better if they are fresh and whole. Bake them on a low heated grill. Do not upturn them. Otherwise, the juices collected during the roasting will leak.

- In order to be delicious grilled meats, fish, and poultry, they need to be left in ***the marinade***. In this way, they become even more palatable.

- Increasingly for baking is used ***aluminum foil***. When wrapping of the products is necessary to provide a sufficiently large foil. Everything should be covered well. The foil shall be coated with vegetable oil or some other kind of fat. In the enclosed foil should always remain some air because, at heat processing, products expand and can damage the foil. Roasting in aluminum foil takes a longer time to cook than roasting the products directly on the grill.

- To stay juicy, roasted meat, poultry, fish, cheese, vegetables, and mushrooms shall not be pricked with a fork, even when you upturn them on the grill. You shall ***use special tongs*** for this purpose. Otherwise, some of their juice will be lost, and products will become dry.

- No matter what is roasting, once it is ready - put it in a saucepan with a lid. So the grilled products will remain juicy and warm.

- Serve the grilled products after 15 minutes on a warm plate or a wooden board.

Some Useful Tips about the Marinades

- Never add salt in the marinade. The salt causes the leakage of juice and blood from the meat products.

- Always use vegetable oil or olive oil. When it comes to the surface, it forms a protective layer.

- The time of staying the products in the marinade and dependents on the brittleness of the meat or fish and their thickness. It ranges from 1 hour to 48 hours.

- Always place the container with the marinade and the meat in a cool place, preferably in a refrigerator.

- The products must be fully immersed in the marinade. Think in advance about how much of marinade to prepare.

Proper sauce

Without proper sauce, the indoor grill is not finished.

- Roast meat or vegetable on the indoor grill, it's a real ritual, and that's why people all over the world love it. Without proper sauce, the indoor grill is not finished.

- The right sauce can turn even simple roast meat, chicken, or fish into exquisite gastronomic pleasure. To the roast meat, it is nice to prepare some sauce, so as not to be too dry the dish.

- You can invent grill sauce yourself, or you can take advantage of the recipes in this book. They are suitable for different types of meat, chicken, fish, etc.

- Meat (chicken, fish, vegetables, cheese, etc.) sauces can be prepared from different products; they enhance the taste and aroma of them.

- Some types of meat are served entirely in sauce, and some are only partially poured.

- For flavor and extra flavor, spices are added to the sauces.

- With the sauces, you can both eat the meat, melted in the bowl with the fragrant mixture, to make it juicier, and smear the meats while baking them.

The Indoor Grill Cookbook

This page intentionally left blank

R. Lazarova

Grilling Recipes

The Indoor Grill Cookbook

This page intentionally left blank

R. Lazarova

1. Marinated Grilled Pork Back Ribs

Servings: 4

Ingredients:

- 3 lb (1,360 g) natural fresh pork back ribs

- 4 onions - cut into halves

For the marinade: 2 cloves garlic - crushed, 3 tablespoons soy sauce, 1 tablespoon honey, 1 tablespoon tomato paste, ¼ cup white wine, 1 teaspoon ground black pepper, 1 pinch nutmeg, 1 pinch ground allspice, 1 pinch cloves, 1 pinch cinnamon, grated peel of 1 lime

Instructions:

In a large glass bowl, combine all marinade ingredients, mix well; add the pork ribs and stir. Then cover them with plastic food wrap and place in the fridge for 4 - 5 hours or overnight. Do not forget to upturn them from time to time. Then drain them well.

Preheat grill for medium heat. Add a small amount of vegetable oil on a folded piece of paper towel, and then carefully grease the grill with the oil.

Place ribs on the grill for 30 - 40 minutes. Turn round them often and smear with the marinade. Remove the ribs from the grill. Place under foil to rest 8 – 9 minutes.

Put the onions on the grill for 8 – 9 minutes. During grilling, smear the onion with marinade.

Serve the pork ribs warm with grilled onion and with a sauce prepared according to a recipe from this book.

2. Grilled Pork Butt Steak

Servings: 4

Ingredients:

- 4 pcs pork butt steak bone-in

- 2 yellow onions - finely chopped

- ground black pepper to taste, salt to taste

Instructions:

Sprinkle pork steak with ground black pepper and chopped onions. Cover them with plastic food wrap and place in the fridge for 1 - 2 hours. Then, remove the onions.

Preheat grill for medium heat. Add a small amount of vegetable oil on a folded piece of paper towel, and then carefully grease the grill with the oil.

Put the steaks on the grill for 20 – 30 minutes. Turn round them often. Salt them at the end of baking. The appearance of the droplets of the juice on the upper surface of the meat indicates that it is baked from one side. (Cooking time will vary from grill to grill as well as based on the thickness of the pork steak. If pork steak is cut an inch (2.5

cm) thick or less, it will need much less cooking time.)

Remove the steak from the grill. Place under aluminum foil to rest 7 - 8 minutes.

Serve the steak warm with garnish fresh or grilled vegetables and grilled mushrooms.

3. *Garlic Glazed Pork Chops*

Servings: 4

Ingredients:

- 4 pcs pork center-cut loin chops boneless

- 3 cloves garlic, crushed

- ½ teaspoon ground black pepper

- 3 tablespoons ketchup

- 3 tablespoons less-sodium soy sauce

- 1 tablespoon honey

- 2 tablespoons vegetable oil

Instructions:

Place crushed garlic, soy sauce, honey, and ketchup in a glass bowl to make a glaze. Mix the mixture vigorously.

Preheat grill for medium heat. Add a small amount of vegetable oil on a folded piece of paper towel, and then carefully grease the grill with the oil.

Place the pork chops on the grill.

Grill until no longer pink in the center about 7 - 9 minutes on per side. Lightly brush glaze onto each side of the chops as they cook.

Serve the steaks warm with grilled vegetables, with a sauce prepared according to a recipe from this book.

4. Spicy Pork Chops Thin

Servings: 4

Ingredients:

- 2.1 lb (950 g) pork sirloin chops thin boneless

- salt to taste

Spices: 1-tablespoon sunflower oil, 1 teaspoon cayenne pepper, 2 teaspoons mustard, 1 teaspoon smoked paprika

Instructions:

Place all spices in a glass bowl. Mix the mixture vigorously. Smear the chops with this mixture.

Preheat grill for medium heat. Add a small amount of vegetable oil on a folded piece of paper towel, and then carefully grease the grill with the oil.

Place chops on the grill. Grill them for 5 minutes on each side. Salt them at the end of grilling. The appearance of the droplets of the juice on the upper surface of the meat indicates that it is ready from one side. Remove the chops from the grill. Place under aluminum foil to rest 5 – 6 minutes.

Serve the pork chops warm with a sauce prepared

according to a recipe from this book.

5. *Grilled Pork Chop with Apple*

Servings: 4

Ingredients:

- 2 lb (910 g) 4 pcs pork center-cut loin chops boneless

- 2 yellow onions, finely chopped

- 1 sour apple, finely chopped

- 2 Roma tomatoes, finely chopped

Spices: 1-teaspoon ground black pepper, 2 tablespoons vegetable oil, 1-tablespoon tomato ketchup, salt to taste, 4 bay leaves

Instructions:

Place each chop on a double aluminum foil. Season with black pepper, salt, and tomato ketchup. Spread on top the mixture of the onion, tomato, 1bay leaf, and apple. Sprinkle with oil. Wrap the chops in the aluminum foil. Preheat grill to medium heat. Place packages on the grill. Cook 30 – 40 minutes.

Serve the chops with foil.

6. Grilled Pork Tenderloin

Servings: 4

Ingredients:

- 1.8 lb (815 g) pork tenderloin boneless

- 1 yellow onion, cut into halves

Spices: 2 teaspoons butter, ground black pepper to taste, salt to taste

Instructions:

Cut the tenderloin into 4 portions. Preheat grill to medium heat. Rub the grill with peeled and cut in half onions. Smear the meat on both sides with butter, put it on the grill. Allow it to be grill 3 - 4 minutes. Turn it, sprinkle with salt and black pepper. Cook the tenderloin on the grill for another 2 - 3 minutes. Then put it on a plate. Put butter on each portion of meat and serve.

You can add a sauce made according to a recipe from this book.

7. Stuffed Pork Tenderloin

Servings: 1

Ingredients:

- 7 oz (200 g) fresh pork tenderloin

- 2 oz (55 g) smoked bacon, finely chopped

- 1 tablespoon olive oil

- 1 shallot, finely chopped

- 1 clove garlic, finely chopped

Spices: ½ tablespoon finely chopped Italian parsley, 5 drops of chili sauce, ground black pepper to taste, salt to taste

Instructions:

Cut the pork tenderloin in length. Hammer it to become thin.

Heat non - stick pan. Saute olive oil, bacon, onion, and garlic in the pan. After 1 minute, add chili sauce, chopped parsley, and black pepper to taste.

Spread stuffing over tenderloin. Roll up tenderloin, ending at the 2-inch border. At both ends, put on a small metal skewer in order not to leak the stuffing (or tie meat with twine to secure shape). Season the meat all over with ground black pepper and salt.

Preheat grill for medium heat. Add a small amount of vegetable oil on a folded piece of paper towel, and then carefully grease the grill with the oil.

Place the stuffed tenderloin on the grill for 20 – 30 minutes. Turn it and cook another 20 – 30 minutes.

Remove the stuffed tenderloin from the grill. Place under aluminum foil to rest 5 – 6 minutes.

Serve the stuffed tenderloin warm. You can add a sauce made according to a recipe from this book.

8. Texas Style Pork Back Ribs

Servings: 4

Ingredients:

- 3.4 lb (1.500 g) fresh baby pork back ribs

- 2 tablespoon Dijon mustard

For the marinade: 1 onion - finely chopped, 3 clove garlic – grated, 2 tablespoons sunflower oil, 1 jalapeno - cleared of the seeds and finely chopped, 1 teaspoon leaves thyme 2 tablespoons brown sugar or honey, 1.5 teaspoons ground black pepper, 2 teaspoons sweet paprika, 1 tablespoon grated lime peel, 1 teaspoon cumin, 1.5 teaspoon sea salt

Instructions:

Combine all ingredients for the marinade in a glass bowl. Stir them well.

Place the ribs on a large tray. Lightly coat rib (all sides) with mustard. Sprinkle ½ of marinade evenly over ribs. Press into the mustard. Then wrap ribs tightly in aluminum foil. Place in the fridge for 2 hours.

Preheat grill for medium heat. Add a small amount of

vegetable oil on a folded piece of paper towel, and then carefully grease the grill with the oil.

Drain ribs well and place them on the grill. Cook the ribs for 30 minutes.

Sprinkle the remaining marinade over the ribs. Place the ribs, meat side down on the grill. Cook ribs 10 minutes. Turn the ribs, so they are meat side up. Continue cooking for about 5 minutes.

Place under foil to rest 6 – 7 minutes. Garnish with grilled vegetables and grilled fresh corn on the cob. You can add a sauce made according to a recipe from this book.

9. Marinated Pork Country Style Ribs Boneless

Servings: 4

Ingredients:

- 2.5 lb (1.150 g) Pork Country Style Ribs Boneless

For the marinade: 0.5 cups spicy tomato catsup, juice of 1 lime, 1 tablespoon raw & unfiltered honey,1 tablespoon Worcestershire sauce, 0.5 teaspoons ground black pepper, 1.5 teaspoon sea salt, 2 clove garlic – grated, 1 tablespoon grated lime peel pork belly

Instructions:

Combine all ingredients for the marinade in a glass bowl, add ribs. Stir them well. Then cover them with plastic food wrap and place in the fridge for 2 - 3 hours or overnight. Do not forget to upturn them from time to time. Then drain them well from the marinade.

Preheat grill for medium heat. Add a small amount of vegetable oil on a folded piece of paper towel, and then carefully grease the grill with the oil.

Place the ribs on the grill for 30 - 40 minutes. Turn round them often and smear with the marinade. Remove the ribs from the grill. Place under foil to rest 6 – 7 minutes.

Serve the ready ribs with potato salad add a sauce made according to a recipe from this book.

10. Pork Skewers with Thyme

Servings: 4

Ingredients:

- 1.5 lb (680 g) pork shoulder, or pork belly

- 4 onions

- 2 green bell peppers

- 8 cherry tomatoes

- 2 tablespoon vegetable oil

- ¼ teaspoon ground black pepper

- 4 – 5 sprigs fresh thyme, 4 – 5 sprigs fresh living oregano

- salt to taste

Instructions:

Cut the meat into cubes of equal size, about 1 inch – 2.5 cm. Cut the onions and peppers in a form suitable for threading on skewers. Place all ingredients (apart from the salt) in a glass bowl. Stir them thoroughly and add the meat. Cover them with plastic food wrap and place in the fridge for 1 hour.

Preheat grill for medium heat. Add a small amount of vegetable oil on a folded piece of paper towel, and then carefully grease the grill with the oil.

Thread the ingredients for skewer by alternating them: meat, onion, meat, green pepper, meat, tomato. Place the skewers on the grill for 20 - 30 minutes, turn round them often. Season with salt at the end of grilling. Transfer to a platter and serve with a sauce made according to a recipe from this book.

11. Pork Skewers with Vegetables

Servings: 4

Ingredients:

- 1.5 lb (680 g) pork shoulder, or pork belly

- 2 onions, cut into quarters

- 1 lb (450 g) sweet mini peppers (mix of red, yellow, orange)

- 9 oz (255 g) grape tomatoes

- salt to taste

For the marinade: ¼ teaspoon ground black pepper, 4 sprigs fresh rosemary, 3 tablespoons vegetable oil, a juice of ½ lemon

Instructions:

Cut the meat into equal-sized cubes, about 1 inch – 2.5 cm. Sprinkle with chopped rosemary and black pepper on all sides. Pour over them with vegetable oil and lemon juice. Stir well, cover them with plastic food wrap and place in the fridge for 2 hours. Then remove the meat from the marinade and dry it.

Preheat grill for medium heat. Add a small amount of vegetable oil on a folded piece of paper towel, and then carefully grease the grill with the oil.

Thread the ingredients for skewer by alternating: onion, whole tomato, meat, whole pepper, meat. Place the skewers on the grill about 15 - 20 minutes, turning them often. Season with salt at the end of grilling. Transfer to a platter and serve with a sauce made according to a recipe from this book.

12. *Spicy Pork Meatballs*

Servings: 4

Ingredients:

- 1.8 lb (815 g) natural pork mince, 20% fat

- 1 sweet onion, finely chopped

- 1 jalapeno, finely chopped

- 1 tablespoon tomato paste

Spices: 1-teaspoon ground cumin, ½-teaspoon ground black pepper, 2 tablespoons finely chopped Italian parsley, 2 tablespoons sprigs fresh oregano, sea salt to taste

Instructions:

In a glass bowl, place all ingredients and spices. Mix well, cover with plastic food wrap and place in the fridge for 2 – 3 hours.

Preheat grill for medium heat. Add a small amount of vegetable oil on a folded piece of paper towel, and then carefully grease the grill with the oil.

Shape the meatballs, giving them an elliptical or oval

shape. Place them on the grill. Grill from each side for 5 minutes, turn with appropriate tongs (in no case, do not use a fork).

Transfer the meatballs to a platter and serve with fresh salad and sauce made according to a recipe from this book.

13. Pork Meatballs with Mustard

Servings: 4

Ingredients:

- 1.8 lb (815 g) natural pork mince, 20% fat

- 1 sweet onion, finely chopped

- 2 yellow onions, cut into halves

- 1 tablespoon Dijon mustard

Spices: 1-teaspoon sweet paprika, ¼ teaspoon ground black pepper, a pinch of ground coriander, 2 tablespoons chopped parsley, a pinch of thyme, salt to taste

Instructions:

In a glass bowl, combine all ingredients and spices. Stir them well. Then cover them with plastic food wrap and place in the fridge for 1 - 2 hours

Preheat grill for medium heat. Add a small amount of vegetable oil on a folded piece of paper towel, and then carefully grease the grill with the oil.

Make 8 pcs meatballs from the finished mixture with

the minced meat. Place them on the grill. Cook the meatballs on each side for 4 – 5 minutes. Turn with appropriate tongs (in no case, do not use a fork). Place the onion on the grill and bake them for 4 – 5 minutes. Serve the pork meatballs with grilled onion, fresh salad, and sauce made according to a recipe from this book.

14. Ginger Meatballs with Parmesan Cheese

Servings: 4

Ingredients:

- 1.8 lb (815 g) natural pork mince, 20% fat

- 2 teaspoons root ginger loose, finely grated

- 1 clove garlic, finely grated

- ¼ red bell pepper, finely chopped

- 1 sweet onion, finely chopped

- 3 tablespoons Parmesan cheese, shredded

Spices: 1 teaspoon smoked sweet paprika, ¼-teaspoon ground black pepper, 2 tablespoons finely chopped Italian parsley

Instructions:

In a bowl, combine all ingredients, spices, and 2 - 3 tablespoons ice-cold water. Cover them with plastic food wrap and place in the fridge for 1 - 2 hours. Then put some oil in your palms and shape the meatballs, give them a round shape.

Preheat grill for medium heat. Add a small amount of

vegetable oil on a folded piece of paper towel, and then carefully grease the grill with the oil.

Place the meatball on the grill. Cook the meatballs on each side for 5 - 6 minutes. Turn with appropriate tongs (in no case, do not use a fork). Serve the meatballs warm with fresh salad and sauce made according to a recipe from this book.

15. Pork and Beef Meatballs

Servings: 4

Ingredients:

- 1 lb (450 g) natural pork mince, 20% fat

- 9 oz (255 g) beef mince, 20% fat

- 1 yellow onion, very chopped finely

- 4 - 5 tablespoons ice-cold water

- 1 tablespoon vegetable oil

Spices: 1-teaspoon cumin, ¼-teaspoon ground black pepper, 1-teaspoon sea salt, 1-teaspoon sweet paprika, 2 tablespoons finely chopped Italian parsley

Instructions:

In a glass bowl, combine all ingredients and spices; mix well. Then cover them with plastic food wrap and place in the fridge for 1 - 2 hours. Make the meatballs by smearing your hands with some mixture of vinegar and cold water. Flatten the meatballs, give them an oval or round shape.

Preheat grill for medium heat. Add a small amount of

vegetable oil on a folded piece of paper towel, and then carefully grease the grill with the oil.

Place the meatballs on the grill for 5 - 6 minutes. Turn with appropriate tongs (in no case, do not use a fork) and cook another 4 - 5 minutes.

Serve the meatballs warm. Garnish with fresh salad and sauce prepared according to the recipes of this book

16. Garlic Butter Beef Steaks

Servings: 4

Ingredients:

- 4 Beef Chuck Eye Steak

- ground black pepper to taste, sea salt to taste

For the garlic butter: 1 tablespoon finely chopped Italian parsley, 1-tablespoon finely chopped shallot, 1- 2 cloves garlic, grated.

Instructions:

For the garlic butter: in small bowl combine ingredients, mix vigorously. Put the garlic butter in the refrigerator.

Preheat grill for medium heat. Add a small amount of vegetable oil on a folded piece of paper towel, and then carefully grease the grill with the oil.

Let steaks sit out at room temperature for 15 minutes. Then pat dry with a paper towel to ensure the perfect sear. Season them with salt and pepper.

Place the steaks on the grill. Flip only once during cook

to give time to form crust. Use a pair of BBQ tongs with a soft-grip handle. Steaks are ready when they easily lift off the grill. Before removing the steaks from the grill, slather that garlic butter all over them (on each about 1 teaspoon of garlic butter).

Allow ready steaks to rest for 5 minutes before slicing and serve.

17. Beef Skewers with Baby Bella Mushroom

Servings: 4

Ingredients:

- 1.8 lb (815 g) Beef Choice Angus Sirloin Kabobs
- 3 tablespoons lemon juice
- 3 tablespoons olive oil
- 1 – 2 red bell pepper
- 8 pcs whole small shallots
- 12 oz (340 g) whole baby Bella mushroom

Spices: ground black pepper and salt to taste

Instructions:

In a glass bowl, combine all ingredients. Stir them well. Cover with plastic food wrap and place in the fridge for 1 hour.

Heat the grill to medium-high. Add a small amount of vegetable oil on a folded piece of paper towel, and then carefully grease the grill with the oil.

Thread the ingredients for skewer by alternating: beef,

shallots, beef, mushroom, beef, and red pepper. Place the skewers on the grill about 15 - 20 minutes, turning them often. Season with salt at the end of grilling. Transfer to a platter and serve with a sauce made according to a recipe from this book.

18. Grilled Beef Sirloin Tip Steak

Servings: 4

Ingredients:

- 1.61 lb (725 g) Beef Sirloin Tip Steak Thin

For a marinade: 2 tablespoon Dijon mustard, 1 tablespoon lime juice, 1 teaspoon garlic – grated, 1 teaspoon smoked paprika, 1 teaspoon dried tarragon

Spices: ground black pepper to taste, sea salt to taste, 1-tablespoon vegetable oil for grill

Instructions:

Mix all ingredients for the marinade in a glass bowl. Stir well.

Season steaks with black pepper and salt to taste. Coat with marinade. Cover and chill for 2 hours. Then let steaks stand at room temperature for 15 minutes

Before heating the grill, brush it with vegetable oil to prevent sticking. Heat the grill to medium heat.

Place the steaks on the grill. Flip only once during cook to give them time to form crust. Use a pair of BBQ tongs with a soft-grip handle. Steaks are ready when they easily lift off the grill.

Cover ready steaks with foil, and let sit for 4 - 5 minutes before serving to allow the juices to settle within the meat.

19. Beef Burger with Cheddar Cheese

Servings: 4

Ingredients:

- 1.3 lb (590 g) ground beef, 85% Lean/15% Fat

- 2 green onion, finely chopped

- 2 cloves garlic, grated (or garlic powder)

- 1 tablespoon Worcestershire sauce

- 1 tablespoon tomato paste

- 4 sliced Cheddar cheese

- 4 Classics Sesame Topped Hamburger Buns

Spices: 1 teaspoon finely chopped thyme, 1 tablespoon finely chopped parsley, ground black pepper to taste, salt to taste

Garnish: green cabbage, lettuce leaves, tomato and parsley

Instructions:

Place the meat in a large glass bowl. Add the green

onion, garlic, Worcestershire sauce, tomatoes paste and all spices. Gently mix everything until just combined. Try not to overmix. Form the mixture into 4 equal patties.

Preheat grill to medium heat. Use Non- flammable cooking spray to grease grill.

Place the patties on the grill for 5 - 6 minutes each side until a crust on both sides. Turn with appropriate tongs (in no case, do not use a fork). In the last minute of grilling, add a slice of Cheddar cheese to each patty and let the cheese melt. Split each bun and place a patty in the middle. Garnish with green cabbage, lettuce leaves, tomato, and parsley.

Place the burgers to a platter and serve with a sauce made according to a recipe from this book.

20. *Thyme & Rosemary Grilled Lamb Ribs*

Servings: 4

Ingredients:

- 3 lb (1.360 g) – 2 pcs racks lamb ribs

- salt to taste

Spices: 5 – 6 sprigs fresh thyme, 4 sprigs fresh rosemary, 3 cloves of garlic – grated, ground black pepper, 4-tablespoons vegetable oil

Instructions:

Place the lamb racks on a large tray. Season well with garlic and pepper on both sides. Drizzle well with olive oil to coat on both sides. Cut the rosemary and thyme. Sprinkle with the chopped fresh herbs all over the racks. Then cover with plastic food wrap and place in the fridge overnight.

Preheat grill to medium heat. Use Non- flammable cooking spray to grease grill.

Take ribs out of the fridge, and brush off the majority of the chopped spices. Then let ribs stand at room temperature for 15 - 20 minutes.

Place the ribs on the grill. Flip only once during cook to give it time to form crust. Use a pair of grill tongs with a soft-grip handle. Lamb's ribs are ready when they easily lift off the grill.

Remove the ribs from the grill. Place under foil to rest 6 – 7 minutes. Then slice, sprinkle with salt.

Serve grilled lamb ribs with fresh vegetable salad and sauce made according to a recipe from this book

21. *Chimichurri Lamb Loin Chop*

Servings: 4

Ingredients:

- 4 pcs Fresh Lamb Loin Chop

Chimichurri sauce: Combine 2 pcs shallot – finely chopped, chile, 4 cloves garlic - crushed 3 tablespoons red wine vinegar, and 1-teaspoon sea salt in a medium bowl. Let sit 10 minutes. Stir in 1 tablespoon finely chopped cilantro, 1 cup finely chopped Italian parsley, and 3 tablespoons fresh chopped oregano. Using a fork, whisk in 2/3 cup sunflower oil. Transfer ½-cup chimichurri to a small bowl. Season with salt and ground black pepper to taste, reserve as sauce.

Instructions:

Place lamb chop in a glass bowl. Toss with remaining chimichurri sauce. Cover with plastic food wrap and chill at least 3 - 4 hours or up to overnight. Then let chop stand at room temperature for 15 minutes.

Remove lamb chop from chimichurri, pat dry, and grill for 10 - 15 minutes, turning them occasionally.

Put spoon reserved chimichurri sauce over grilled lamb chops. Serve the lamb chops warm.

22. *Spicy Lamb Meatballs*

Servings: 4

Ingredients:

- 1.8 lb (815 g) lamb mince, 15 % fat

Spices: 1½ teaspoon ground cumin, ½-teaspoon coriander, ½ teaspoon crushed red pepper, 1 tablespoon finely chopped fresh mint, 1/3 teaspoon ground black pepper, sea salt to taste

Instructions:

Place the minced meat and all spices in a large glass bowl. Gently mix everything, adding a little cold water until mixture smooth and elastic. Divide the mixture into 8 equal parts. Shape 8 round-shaped meatballs.

Heat grill to medium-high. Add a small amount of vegetable oil on a folded piece of paper towel, and then carefully grease the grill with the oil.

Place the meatballs on the grill. Use a pair of grill tongs with a soft-grip handle. Grill lamb meatballs about 4 – 5 minutes each side until a crust on both sides.

Serve the meatballs warm with fresh salad and sauce homemade according to a recipe of this book.

23. Lamb Skewers

Servings: 4

Ingredients:

- 1.8 lb (815 g) lamb boneless shoulder

- 2 onions, finely chopped

- 2 cloves garlic, grated

- juice of ½ lemon

- 3 sprigs fresh rosemary

Spices: ground black pepper to taste, salt to taste

Instructions:

Cut the meat into equal-sized cubes, about 1 inch – 2.5 cm. Place it in a glass bowl. Combine the meat with the onion, garlic, lemon juice, and rosemary. Stir them well. Cover with plastic food wrap and chill at least 1 - 2 hours or up to overnight. Then carefully remove the spices from the meat. String the meat on skewers. Then let stand at room temperature for 15 minutes. Sprinkle with pepper and salt.

Heat grill to medium-high. Add a small amount of

vegetable oil on a folded piece of paper towel, and then carefully grease the grill with the oil.

Place the skewers on the grill. Cook on one side for 3 minutes. Flip over and cook another 3 minutes. Cook on the remaining sides for 1 minute per side. Allow ready meat to rest for 5 minutes before serving. Add sauce (prepared according to a recipe of this book) and fresh vegetable salad.

24. Mediterranean Style Lamb Kebabs

Servings: 4

Ingredients:

- 1.8 lb (815 g) lamb shoulder

- green, orange, and red bell pepper, cut into 1 inch (2.5 cm) pieces

- 2 sweet onion, cut into quarters

Spices: ground black pepper to taste, salt to taste, lime for decoration

For the marinade: 5 – 6 sprigs fresh Italian parsley, 3 – 4 sprigs fresh oregano, juice of ½ lime, 2 cloves garlic - grated, sea salt to taste, ground black pepper to taste, 4 tablespoons vegetable oil

Instructions

Cut the meat into equal-sized cubes, about 1 inch – 2.5 cm. Combine the marinade ingredients in a blender. Pulse for a few seconds until smooth mix. Place the lamb meat and marinade in a glass bowl. Stir gently so the meat will taste better. Cover with plastic food wrap and chill at least 2 – 3 hours.

Heat the grill to medium-high. Add a small amount of vegetable oil on a folded piece of paper towel, and then carefully grease the grill with the oil.

Place a cube of lamb on a skewer, followed by the peppers and onions. Repeat until the skewers are filled. Place the skewers on the grill. Grill the lamb kebabs for 8 minutes to the desired doneness, turning the skewers every 1 to 2 minutes. Sprinkle generously with salt and pepper and serve with fresh vegetable salad and sauce made according to a recipe from this book.

25. Lamb and Beef Burger

Servings: 4

Ingredients:

- 1 lb (450 g) lamb mince, fat 15 %

- 9 oz (255 g) minced beef, fat 5 %

Spices: 1½-teaspoon ground cumin, ground black pepper and salt to taste, 4 cloves garlic - crushed, 1 cup ice - cold water

Instructions:

Combine the meat with the spices, as the dough is kneaded. Prepare a mixture of 1 part wine vinegar and two parts cold water. Form the mixture into 4 equal patties.

Heat the grill to medium-high. Add a small amount of vegetable oil on a folded piece of paper towel, and then carefully grease the grill with the oil. Place the patties on the grill. Use a pair of grill tongs with a soft-grip handle. Grill patties about 5 minutes each side until a crust on both sides. Put the cheddar cheese on the patties 1 – 2 minutes before removing them from the grill.

Put the ready patties in burger buns. Garnish with fresh vegetables (tomato, cucumber, cabbage, lettuce) and sauce.

You can garnish with homemade sauce according to the recipes of this book.

26. Lamb & Sausage Skewers

Servings:

Ingredients:

- 1.3 lb (590 g) lamb from the shoulder

- 8 oz (225 g) 2 links hot Italian sausage

- 2 onions

- 2 red bell peppers

Spices: ground black pepper to taste, salt to taste, a lump of butter

Instructions:

Cut the onions, peppers, and sausage on pieces suitable for threading on skewers.

Cut the lamb into cubes of equal size (1 - 1.2 inch / 2.5 - 3 cm). Put meat in a glass bowl. Add the marinade and mix well. (Prepare the marinade according to a recipe from this book). Cover it with plastic food wrap and place in the fridge for 2 hours. Then pat dry with a paper towel.

Heat the grill to medium-high. Add a small amount of

vegetable oil on a folded piece of paper towel, and then carefully grease the grill with the oil.

Place a cube of meat on a skewer, followed by the onion, sausage, pepper, meat, onion, sausage. Repeat until the skewers are filled. Season with salt and pepper. Place the skewers on the grill. Cook on one side for 3 minutes. Flip over and cook another 3 minutes. Cook on the remaining sides for 1 minute per side. Allow ready meat to rest for 5 minutes before serving.

You can add homemade sauce according to the recipes of this book.

27. Grilled Juicy Fresh Sausages

Servings: 4

Ingredients:

- 2 x 19 oz (1.077 g) fresh sausages (choose your favorite sausages: beef, pork, Italian....)

Instructions:

First, drop sausages into boiling liquid long enough to tighten the skin.

Heat the grill to medium-high. Add a small amount of vegetable oil on a folded piece of paper towel, and then carefully grease the grill with the oil.

Place the sausages on a hot grill and finish cooking for 15 minutes. Turn them over 2 - 3 times. Use a pair of grill tongs with a soft-grip handle.

This method gives you juicy sausages. It's one sure way to keep the casings from hardening.

Serve the sausages warm. You can add homemade sauce according to the recipes of this book.

28. Grilled Chicken Breast

Servings: 4

Ingredients:

4 pcs fresh boneless, skinless chicken breasts

Spices: ground black pepper to taste, sea salt to taste

For a marinade: 5 – leaves fresh sage, 1 stick fresh lemongrass and 3 – 4 sprigs fresh thyme (or ½ tablespoon mix of dried herbs), 1 tablespoon Worcestershire sauce, 3 tablespoons olive oil, Juice of 1 lime, 2 tablespoons balsamic vinegar, 1 tablespoon honey, 1 tablespoon brown sugar, 1 tablespoon mustard, 2 cloves garlic - grated

Instructions:

Finely chop the fresh herbs. Put them in a large glass bowl. Add the other ingredients for the marinade. Stir well. Save in a small bowl ¼ part of the marinade. Combine in the large bowl the chicken breasts and 3/4 part of the marinade. Cover with plastic food wrap and place in the fridge for 2 hours to overnight. Then drain the chicken breasts from the marinade.

Heat grill to medium-high heat. Add a small amount of vegetable oil on a folded piece of paper towel, and then carefully grease the grill with the oil.

Sprinkle chicken breast with black pepper and sea salt. Place them on to grill (or grill pan). Grill it about 5 - 6 minutes each side. Use a pair of grill tongs with a soft-grip handle.

Serve the chicken breast with garnish and sauce made according to a recipe from this book.

29. Grilled Chicken Drumstick

Servings: 4

Ingredients:

- 8 pcs fresh chicken drumstick

For a marinade: 1 onion – finely chopped, 2 cloves garlic – grated, 1 teaspoon smoked red paprika, ¼ teaspoon ground black pepper, sea salt to taste, peel of 1 lemon, 1 tablespoon vegetable oil

Instructions:

Combine in a small glass bowl all ingredients for the marinade. Stir well. Sprinkle each chicken drumstick on all sides. Let rest at room temperature 15 minutes.

Heat grill to medium-high heat. Add a small amount of vegetable oil on a folded piece of paper towel, and then carefully grease the grill with the oil.

Place the chicken drumstick on the grill for 30 - 35 minutes, flip every 5 minutes. Use a pair of grill tongs with a soft-grip handle. Remove the chicken drumstick from the grill. Place under foil to rest 6 – 7 minutes.

You can add homemade sauce according to the recipes of this book.

30. Grilled Flattened Chicken

Servings: 4

Ingredients:

- 1 pcs fresh whole chicken, about 3 – 4 lb (1.360 – 1.800 g)

Dry marinade: 1/3 teaspoon ground black pepper, 1 teaspoon sea salt, ¼ teaspoon turmeric powder, 1 teaspoon cumin ground, pinch of nutmeg ground, 1 teaspoon smoked paprika, pinch of ground ginger, ¼ teaspoon coriander ground, grated peel of 1 orange

Instructions:

Remove and discard giblets and neck from chicken. Rinse chicken with cold water. Then pat dry with a paper towel. Trim excess fat.

Place chicken, breast side down, on a cutting surface. Cut chicken in half lengthwise along the backbone, cutting to, but not through, other side. Turn chicken over. Starting at the neck cavity, loosen skin from breast and drumsticks by inserting fingers, gently pushing between skin and meat. Place chicken, breast side up, in a baking tray.

The Indoor Grill Cookbook

Make the dry marinade. Combine in a glass bowl all ingredients and stir well.

Pour it under the skin and over the surface of the chicken. Cover it with plastic food wrap and place in the fridge for 2 hours to overnight. Then let rest at room temperature 15 minutes.

Heat grill to medium-high heat. Add a small amount of vegetable oil on a folded piece of paper towel, and then carefully grease the grill with the oil. Cook the chicken skin side down, and weight the chicken down with aluminum foil bricks, or the same baking dish you marinated the chicken in. Cook for 25 minutes, and then flip the chicken, so it is skin side up. Put the brick or baking dish back on the chicken. Continue cooking about 30 - 40 minutes more, depending on the size of the chicken.

Let the chicken for 7 – 8 minutes before serving.

You can make sauce according to the recipes of this book.

31. *Stuffed Chicken Breast*

Servings: 4

Ingredients:

- 4 fresh boneless skinless chicken breast fillets

- 7 oz (200 g) fresh young spinach leaves, washed

- 3 tablespoons vegetable oil

Spices: 1 teaspoon grated garlic, 4 – 5 fresh leaves mint, fresh rosemary to taste, 1 tablespoon finely chopped parsley, ground black pepper to taste, sea salt to taste

Instructions:

Cut each chicken breast, so as to form a pocket. In a hot pan, add vegetable oil and saute spinach and garlic for 1 - 2 minutes. Season with all spices. Stuff the chicken breasts. Sew them together with string or secure it with toothpicks.

Heat grill to medium-high heat. Add a small amount of vegetable oil on a folded piece of paper towel, and then carefully grease the grill with the oil.

Place the chicken on the grill for 6 - 7 minutes on each side. Let for 5 minutes before serving.

The rest of the spinach mixture place on the bottom of a serving plate; arrange the chicken breasts on top.

You can add homemade sauce according to the recipes of this book.

32. Lemon Marinade Chicken Skewers with Bacon

Servings: 4

Ingredients:

- 1.7 lb (770 g) boneless, skinless fresh chicken breast

- 12 oz (340 g) smoked bacon, sliced

For the lemon marinade: 4 - 5 tablespoons vegetable oil, juice of 1 lemon, grated zest of 1 lemon, 1 tablespoon chopped parsley, 1 tablespoon fresh oregano, 2 green chopped onion

Instructions:

Combine in a glass bowl all ingredients for the lemon marinade and stir well.

Cut the chicken on cubes of equal size (1 - 1.2 inch/ 2.5 - 3 cm). Place it in a deep bowl together with the marinade. Cover with plastic food wrap and place in the fridge for 2 hours to overnight, stirring occasionally. Then drained chicken, let rest at room temperature 15 minutes.

Wrap each chicken piece with bacon. String them on skewers.

Heat grill to medium-high heat. Add a small amount of vegetable oil on a folded piece of paper towel, and then carefully grease the grill with the oil.

Place the chicken skewers on the grill for 15 – 20 minutes. Turn over every 3 minutes and each time and brush with marinade. Let for 5 minutes before serving.

Serve the chicken skewers with a garnish of fresh or roasted vegetables and sauce prepared according to a recipe from this book.

33. Grilled Turkey Breast

Servings: 4

Ingredients:

- 1.8 lb (815 g) fresh boneless, skinless turkey breast

- Sea salt to taste

For the marinade: 2 cloves garlic - grated, 3 tablespoons white wine, 3 tablespoons olive oil, juice of ½ orange, oregano leaves to taste, 2 teaspoons brown sugar, ground black pepper to taste

Instructions:

In a small glass bowl, mix the black pepper, garlic, and oregano. Rub over the turkey breasts. In a large deep bowl, blend white wine, olive oil, orange juice, and brown sugar. Place the breasts in the bowl, and turn to coat. Cover it with plastic food wrap and marinate in the refrigerator for 3 hours to overnight.

Heat grill to medium-high heat. Add a small amount of vegetable oil on a folded piece of paper towel, and then carefully grease the grill with the oil.

Discard marinade. Remove meat, drain it well and let rest at room temperature 15 minutes. Then place it on the grill. Cook about 5 - 6 minutes on each side, until it is no pink color remains.

Let for 5 minutes before serving. Season with salt to taste. You can choose sauce according to a recipe from this book.

34. Spicy Turkey Burger

Servings: 4

Ingredients:

- 21 oz (600 g) turkey thigh mince, 7% fat

Spices: 1 clove garlic, grated, 1 jalapeno pepper, finely chopped,1 tablespoon Worcestershire sauce, 2 tablespoons freshly chopped Italian parsley, ½ teaspoon freshly ground black pepper, 1 teaspoon sea salt

For the sauce: 2 tablespoons mayonnaise, 2 tablespoons yogurt, 2 tablespoons grated mozzarella cheese, ½ teaspoon curry, 1 clove of garlic grated

For the burger: 4 burger buns, 4 lettuce leaves, tomato - 4 discs, sauce

Instructions:

First, prepare the sauce. Mix all the ingredients in a bowl. Stir vigorously. Store the sauce in a refrigerator.

In a large glass bowl, mix turkey and all spices. Form the mixture into 4 equal flat patties.

Preheat grill to medium heat. Use Non- flammable

cooking spray to grease grill.

Place patties on the grill and cook 5 – 6 minutes per side. Split each bun and place a patty in the middle. Garnish with sauce, lettuce, tomato, and sprig fresh parsley.

35. *Grilled White Fish*

Servings: 4

Ingredients:

- 1.5 lb (680 g) white fish fillet (halibut, cod or other fish of your choice)

Spices: grated peel of 1 lime, ground black pepper to taste, sea salt to taste, 1 tablespoon sunflower oil, juice of ½ lime

Instructions:

Rinse the fish and dry with paper towels. Place it in a glass bowl. Seasonal with a peel of lime, black pepper, salt, oil, and juice of the lime. Stir, cover with plastic food wrap and refrigerate for 1 hour.

Preheat grill to medium heat. Add a small amount of vegetable oil on a folded piece of paper towel, and then carefully grease the grill with the oil.

Place the fish on the grill with the skin. Cook about for 7 – 8 minutes on each side, or until the fish should no longer be opaque in the center.

Transfer the fish to plates. You can choose a sauce for fish according to a recipe from this book.

36. Salmon Burger with Whole Wheat Buns

Servings: 4

Ingredients:

- 21 oz (600 g) fresh skinless & boneless salmon fillet

- 2 green onion

- 1 clove garlic, crushed

- 1 teaspoon tomato paste

- 4 whole-wheat hamburger buns

- garnish - lettuce leaves, tomato, avocado, and red onion; sauce

Spices: grated zest of 1 lime, 1 tablespoon lime juice, 1 tablespoon finely chopped Italian parsley, 1 tablespoon finely chopped dill, ground black pepper to taste, salt to taste

Instructions:

Cut salmon fillet into pieces. Place them in a food chopper for 2 – 3 seconds (grind them, being careful not to make a mess). Place the minced fish in a large bowl. Add the finely chopped onion, crushed garlic, tomato paste, and spices.

Form mixture into 4 equal patties.

Preheat grill to medium heat. Use Non- flammable cooking spray to grease grill.

Grill fish patties until a crust on both sides (about 5 – 6 minutes each side).

Slice the buns into two halves. Garnish with lettuce leaves, tomato, avocado, and red onion. You can choose sauce according to a recipe from this book.

37. Fish Burger with Cheddar Cheese

Servings: 4

Ingredients:

- 21 oz (600 g) loch trout fillet (or other white fish)

- 1 clove garlic, grated (or garlic powder)

- 1 teaspoon Worcestershire sauce

- ½ tablespoon non- pareille capers

- 1 teaspoon tomato paste

- 4 sliced Cheddar cheese

- 4 Classics Sesame Topped Hamburger Buns

- garnish - green cabbage, lettuce leaves, tomato, and parsley; sauce

Spices: 1 teaspoon finely chopped thyme, 1 tablespoon finely chopped parsley, ground black pepper to taste, salt to taste

Instructions:

Remove the skin of the fish fillet. Cut it into pieces.

Place in a food chopper for 2 - 3 seconds (grind, being careful not to make a mess). Place the ground fish in a large glass bowl. Add grated garlic, Worcestershire sauce, capers, tomato paste, and spices. Form mixture into 4 equal patties.

Preheat grill to medium heat. Use Non- flammable cooking spray to grease grill.

Grill fish patties until a crust on both sides (about 5 – 6 minutes each side). In the last minute of grilling, add a slice of Cheddar cheese to fish patties, cover with aluminum foil, and let the cheese melt. Split each bun and place fish patties in the middle. Garnish with green cabbage, lettuce leaves, tomato, and parsley. You can choose sauce according to a recipe from this book.

38. Grilled Whole Sea Fish

Servings: 1

Ingredients:

- 1 whole small fresh sea fish (Sea Bass, Sea Bream, Mackerel)

Spices: Juice of ½ lemon, crushed sea salt to taste, ground black pepper to taste, 1-tablespoon olive oil

Instructions:

Clean the fish, removing, and vertebral bone. Pour the sea fish with freshly squeezed lemon juice, and rub the inside with salt and ground black pepper. Cover it with plastic food wrap. Allow standing for 30 minutes in the refrigerator.

Preheat grill to medium heat. Use Non- flammable cooking spray to grease grill.

Brush the sea fish with olive oil inside and out. Place it on the grill. Cook about 12 - 15 minutes on each side.

Serve the grilled fish with fresh vegetables. You can choose sauce according to a recipe from this book.

39. Wild Caught Cod Fillet

Servings: 4

Ingredients:

- 1.3 lb (590 g) wild-caught Icelandic cod fillet (or sea bream fillet)

- 1 tablespoon olive oil

- 1 tablespoon tomato paste

Spices: 4 slices of lemon, sea salt to taste, ground black pepper to taste

Instructions:

Sprinkle the fish fillet with salt and pepper. Allow standing for 15 minutes in the refrigerator.

Preheat grill to medium heat. Use Non- flammable cooking spray to grease grill. Dilute the tomato paste with 1-tablespoon water and add the olive oil. Stir the mixture well. Dip each fillet in this mixture. Place it on the grill. Cook about 5 - 7 minutes on each side.

Serve the fish with slices of lemon, grilled potatoes, and sauce prepared according to a recipe from this book.

40. Grilled Halibut Fillet

Servings: 4

Ingredients:

- 1.8 lb (810 g) fresh halibut fillet

For the marinade: 3 tablespoons vegetable oil, 2 - 3 tablespoons lemon juice, 3 cloves garlic - finely chopped, 1 tablespoon finely chopped fresh dill, 1 teaspoon fresh thyme, 1 teaspoon fresh rosemary, salt to taste, ground black pepper to taste

Instructions:

Combine in a glass bowl all ingredients for the marinade and stir well. Rub the fish with the marinade. Cover it with plastic food wrap. Let it for 1 hour in the refrigerator. Then drain the fish, discarding the marinade.

Preheat grill to medium heat. Use Non- flammable cooking spray to grease grill. Place fish on the grill for 6 – 7 minutes on each side.

Serve the fish with fresh salad and sauce prepared according to a recipe from this book.

41. Mackerel with Fennel

Servings: 4

Ingredients:

- 4 x 6.5 oz (4 x 180 g) fresh mackerel fillets

- 1 pcs fresh fennel, cut into very thin slices

Spices: 2 tablespoons freshly chopped fresh Italian parsley, 2 - 3 tablespoons vegetable oil, salt to taste, ground black pepper to taste, 3 tablespoons lemon juice

Instructions:

Preheat grill to medium heat. Add a small amount of vegetable oil on a folded piece of paper towel, and then carefully grease the grill with the oil.

Rinse the fish and dry it thoroughly with a paper towel. Season with black pepper and salt. Place the fish fillet on the grill for 6 – 7 minutes on each side (first with the skin underneath).

Season fennel with lemon juice, vegetable oil, salt, and parsley. Spread it in an even layer in an oblong dish. Place the fish fillets on the fennel and serve. You can use the sauce for fish according to a recipe from this book.

42. Grilled Sardines

Servings: 4

Ingredients:

- 20 – 24 medium or large sardines, cleaned

Spices: 2 tablespoons olive oil, salt to taste, ground black pepper to taste, lemon wedges, 4 – 5 fresh rosemary sprigs

Instructions:

Rinse the fish and dry with paper towels. Toss with the olive oil and season with salt and black pepper.

Preheat grill to medium heat. Add a small amount of vegetable oil on a folded piece of paper towel, and then carefully grease the grill with the oil. When the grill is ready, toss the rosemary sprigs. After 1 - 2 minutes, place the sardines in batches if necessary. Grill for a 2 on each side, depending on the size. Transfer from the grill to a platter using tongs or a wide metal spatula.

Serve with lemon wedges. You can use a sauce for fish according to a recipe from this book.

43. Garlic Trout

Servings: 4

Ingredients:

- 4 fresh trout fillets (about 1.8 lb – 815 g)

For the marinade: 4 tablespoons olive oil, 2 tablespoons apple cider vinegar, 1 – 2 cloves garlic - grated, a pinch of ground sage, a pinch of crumbled rosemary, ground black pepper to taste, salt to taste

Instructions:

In a small saucepan, heat the olive oil on low heat. Add garlic, sage, and rosemary, stir well about 1 – 2 minutes. Remove from the heat and immediately add apple cider vinegar, salt, and black pepper. Let the marinade to cold.

Place the fish in a glass bowl. Sprinkle it with salt to taste. Add ½ of the marinade and turn to coat.

Preheat grill to medium heat. Add a small amount of vegetable oil on a folded piece of paper towel, and then carefully grease the grill with the oil. Place the fish fillet skin-side down for 2 minutes. Turn and cook 3 – 4 minutes. Serve fish warm, pour on it ½ of the marinade. Garnish with fresh vegetables.

44. Salmon Skewers

Servings: 4

Ingredients:

- 1.3 lb (590 g) boneless, skinless fresh salmon fillet

- 2 yellow onions

- 1 green bell peppers

- 1 red bell peppers

- 4 lemon wedges

For the marinade: 3 tablespoons olive oil, juice of ½ lemon, 2 cloves garlic- grated, 2 tablespoons fresh dill – finely chopped, a pinch of lovage, a pinch of sea salt

Instructions:

Cut the fish on cubes of equal size (1 - 1.2 inch/ 2.5 - 3 cm). Combine in a glass bowl all ingredients for the marinade. Stir in the salmon season and put in the fridge to marinate for 30 minutes.

Cut the onion and peppers into pieces for skewers.

Preheat grill to medium heat. Add a small amount of

vegetable oil on a folded piece of paper towel, and then carefully grease the grill with the oil.

Thread 3 - 4 pieces of salmon, 1 piece of onion, 1 piece of red pepper, 1 piece of green pepper into each skewer. Cook on the grill for 5- 6 minutes, turning regularly, or until the salmon and vegetables are cooked through.

Serve salmon skewers warm with lemon wedges.

45. White Fish Cakes

Servings: 4

Ingredients:

- 26 oz (740 g) boneless, skinless fish fillet or fish ground (hake, cod, tilapia, halibut)

- 1 tablespoon vegetable oil

- 1 onion, finely chopped

- 2 cloves of garlic, grated

- 1 egg

- 1 - 2 tablespoon breadcrumbs

Spices: ½-teaspoon ground black pepper, 2 tablespoons finely chopped fresh parsley, 1-tablespoon fresh thyme, sea salt to taste

Instructions:

If you are using fish fillet, whizz it in the food processor for 2 - 3 seconds (grind them, being careful not to make a mess). Place the ground fish in a large glass bowl. Add grated garlic, onion, egg, and all spices. With oiled hands, form 8 equal cakes.

Preheat grill to medium heat. Use Non- flammable cooking spray to grease grill.

Cook the fish cakes until a crust on both sides (about 5 – 6 minutes each side).

Serve fish cakes with fresh vegetable salad. You can use sauce according to a recipe from this book.

46. Shrimp Skewers

Servings: 4

Ingredients:

- 1.5 lb (680 g) raw jumbo shrimp peeled and deveined

- 4 lemon wedges

- 1 tablespoon finely chopped fresh dill

For the marinade: 4 tablespoons olive oil, Juice of ½ lime, 4 tablespoons white wine, grated peel of ½ lime, 1 grated clove garlic, ½ teaspoon fish & seafood seasonings

Instructions:

In a deep glass bowl, blend all ingredients for the marinade. Place the shrimp in the bowl and stir to combine. Cover it with plastic food wrap and marinate in the refrigerator for 15 – 20 minutes.

Heat a grill or grill pan over medium-high heat. Add a small amount of vegetable oil on a folded piece of paper towel, and then carefully grease the grill with the oil.

Remove shrimps and drain them well. Discard marinade. Thread the shrimp onto skewers. Place the skewers on the grill. Cook for 2 minutes on each side or until shrimp is pink and opaque. Sprinkle with fresh dill and serve with lemon wedges. You can choose sauce according to a recipe from this book.

47. Grilled Mozzarella Cheese

Servings: 4

Ingredients:

- 17 oz (480 g) whole milk Mozzarella cheese
- 2 teaspoons butter
- 1 green bell peppers
- 4 cherry tomatoes, cut into of halves

Spices: 1 teaspoon smoked paprika, ground black pepper to taste, 8 fresh basil leaves, 1-tablespoon sunflower oil

Instructions:

Prepare 4 sheets of aluminum foil, coated with oil. Cut the cheese into 4 pieces. Sprinkle one side with black pepper, the other with smoked paprika. On each sheet of foil put a piece of cheese. On both sides, put 1 piece green pepper, 2 halves of cherry tomato, 2 leaves fresh basil at the top ½-teaspoon butter. Form tight packages. Immerse the packages in water for 2 – 3 seconds.

Preheat grill to medium heat. Use Non- flammable cooking spray to grease grill.

Place packages on the grill. Cook the cheese for about 7 – 8 minutes each side. Serve each package in a separate plate and open it carefully.

48. Grilled Fresh Portabella Mushroom

Servings: 4

Ingredients:

- 12 oz (340 g) fresh large portabella mushroom

- 2 teaspoons butter

Spices: ¼-teaspoon ground black pepper, juice of ½ lemon, sea salt to taste

Instructions:

Using a damp paper towel or mushroom brush wipe mushrooms of any visible dirt. Remove stems.

Heat a grill or grill pan over medium-high heat. Add a small amount of vegetable oil on a folded piece of paper towel, and then carefully grease the grill with the oil.

Sprinkle the caps with black pepper. Place them on the grill. Cook the mushroom for 10 - 15 minutes. Serve them with melted butter. Sprinkle with salt and lemon juice.

You can choose sauce according to a recipe from this book.

49. *Stuffed Mushroom with Cheddar Cheese*

Servings: 4

Ingredients:

- 1.1 lb (500 g) fresh large flat mushroom

- 8.5 oz (240 g) mild Cheddar cheese slices

- 1 teaspoon butter

- 2 cloves garlic, crushed

- 2 – 3 tablespoon Panko crumbs

Spices: 5 – 6 sprigs fresh thyme, 1 tablespoon finely chopped parsley, ground black pepper, salt to taste

Instructions:

Using a damp paper towel or mushroom brush wipe mushrooms of any visible dirt and remove stems. Chop them into small pieces. Put in a non-stick pan the butter. Add the chopped stems, garlic, salt, and black pepper and cook until the water evaporates. Then add thyme, parsley, and panko crumbs. Mix until well combined. Let the mixture cool.

Fill mushroom caps with cool mixture. You can use a small cream scoop. Then pressed down lightly so you can get more filling in. Put 1 – 2 cheese slices on each stuffed mushroom.

Heat a grill or grill pan over medium-high heat. Add a small amount of vegetable oil on a folded piece of paper towel, and then carefully grease the grill with the oil.

Place mushroom caps on to the grill. Cook for about 20 minutes. You can choose sauce according to a recipe from this book.

50. Grilled Fresh Vegetables

Servings: 4

Ingredients:

- 4 Roma tomato, cut into halves
- 2 orange bell peppers, cut into 4 slices by length (remove seeds)
- 1 eggplant, cut into 8 slices by length
- 2 zucchini, cut into 6 slices by length
- 2 sweet onions, cut into halves
- 2 tablespoons olive oil

Spices: salt to taste, 2 tablespoons finely chopped Italian parsley

Instructions:

Heat a grill or grill pan over medium-high heat. Add a small amount of vegetable oil on a folded piece of paper towel, and then carefully grease the grill with the oil.

Sprinkle the chopped vegetables with salt to taste. Let to drain for about 15 minutes. Dry them with paper towels. Place the vegetables on the grill. Cook for 15 minutes. Turn the vegetables except for the tomato and the onion. Pour with oil and cook another 10 – 15 minutes. In each serving plate, place a few pieces of each vegetable, sprinkle with parsley.

You can choose a sauce for vegetables according to a recipe from this book.

51. Skewered Grilled Potatoes

Servings: 4

Ingredients:

- 1.5 lb (680 g) fresh baby yellow potatoes

- 4 cloves of garlic, grated

- 6 tablespoons olive oil or vegetable oil

- grated peel of 1 lemon

- juice of 1 lemon

Spices: 1-tablespoon fresh thyme, ground black pepper to taste, salt to taste, 2 tablespoons finely chopped parsley

Instructions:

Place potatoes, hot water, and salt in a stockpot with lid. Cook the potatoes for about 8 minutes. Drain potatoes and allow steaming for 5 – 6 minutes to dry.

In a deep glass bowl, stir together olive oil, lemon juice, grated lemon peel, grated garlic, and thyme. Mix in drained potatoes and toss to coat. Cover it with plastic food wrap and marinate in the refrigerator for 50 - 60 minutes.

Heat a grill over medium-high heat. Add a small

amount of vegetable oil on a folded piece of paper towel, and then carefully grease the grill with the oil.

Remove potatoes from marinade. Thread the potatoes onto skewers. Place on the grill for 8 – 10 minutes, occasionally brushing with marinade, turning halfway through. Potatoes should remain crunchy. Remove them from skewers. Sprinkle with black pepper, parsley, and serve hot. You can choose sauce according to a recipe from this book.

52. Vegetable Skewers with Croutons

Servings: 4

Ingredients:

- 2 fresh zucchini

- 16 cherry tomatoes

- 1 garlic

- 2 red onions, cut into pieces

- 1 bread (baguette), cut into cubes

- 3 tablespoons olive oil

- 8 – 12 bay leaves

Spices: ½-tablespoon thyme, ground black pepper to taste, salt to taste

Instructions:

Cut the zucchini into cubes. Peel the garlic and the onion. Prepare the skewers by consistently stringing the zucchini, onion, tomato, clove of garlic, bread, bay leaf. Sprinkle with salt and pepper. Smear the skewers with olive oil and sprinkle them with thyme.

Heat a grill over medium-high heat. Add a small

amount of vegetable oil on a folded piece of paper towel, and then carefully grease the grill with the oil.

Place skewers on the grill for 10 minutes, turning halfway through. Vegetables should remain crunchy. You can choose a sauce for vegetables according to a recipe from this book.

53. *Whole Mushroom Skewers*

Servings: 4

Ingredients:

- 1.5 lb (680 g) whole baby mushrooms

- 1 tablespoon butter, melted

- 2 cloves of garlic, crushed

- 2 tablespoons olive oil

- 4 tablespoons lemon juice

Spices: 1 tablespoon finely chopped fresh dill, 1 tablespoon finely chopped Italian parsley, ground black pepper to taste, salt to taste

Instructions:

Using a damp paper towel or mushroom brush wipe mushrooms of any visible dirt. Smear them with lemon juice. In a large glass bowl, combine olive oil, butter – melted, garlic, dill, and black pepper. Add whole baby mushrooms and toss to coat. Thread mushrooms onto skewers. Reserving any remaining mixture with butter.

Heat a grill over medium-high heat. Add a small amount of vegetable oil on a folded piece of paper towel, and

then carefully grease the grill with the oil.

Place the skewers on the grill, turning occasionally and brushing with reserved butter mixture until mushrooms are tender - about 8 – 10 minutes.

Sprinkle with salt and parsley. Serve with homemade sauce according to a recipe from this book.

54. *Vegetarian Skewers*

Servings: 4

Ingredients:

- 1 small eggplant, cut into cubes

- 1 large green zucchini, cut into cubes

- 7oz (200 g) whole mini portabella mushrooms

- 2 sweet onions

- 2 red bell pepper, cut into pieces for skewers

- 2 tablespoons finely chopped parsley

- a pinch of sea salt

For the marinade: a juice of ½ lemon, 3 tablespoons olive oil, ½ teaspoon sweet paprika, 2 – 3 fresh sprig of thyme, 1 fresh sprig rosemary, a pinch of ground black pepper

Instructions:

Using a damp paper towel or mushroom brush wipe mushrooms of any visible dirt. Smear them with lemon juice. In a glass bowl, mix all ingredients for the marinade.

Heat a grill over medium-high heat. Add a small amount of vegetable oil on a folded piece of paper towel, and

then carefully grease the grill with the oil.

Remove vegetables and mushrooms from marinade. Thread them onto skewers. Place skewers on the grill for 10 – 15 minutes, occasionally brushing with marinade.

Sprinkle with salt and parsley. Serve with homemade sauce according to a recipe from this book.

55. *Stuffed Skewers Tomato*

Servings: 4

Ingredients:

- 8 small tomatoes

- 8 small pieces of feta cheese or mozzarella cheese

- 1 sweet onion, cut into quarters

- 2 green bell peppers, cut into pieces

- 1 tablespoon vegetable oil

- sea salt to taste

For stuffing: 8 small pieces of feta cheese, 1 clove crushed garlic, a pinch of ground black pepper, 1 teaspoon fresh finely chopped oregano, 1 tablespoon vegetable oil

Instructions:

In a small glass bowl, mix all ingredients for stuffing.

Wash the tomatoes and cut them small lids. Carefully remove their inside. Stuff the tomatoes. Sprinkle the bell peppers and onion with salt.

Heat a grill over medium-high heat. Add a small amount of vegetable oil on a folded piece of paper towel, and

then carefully grease the grill with the oil.

Thread by alternating pepper, stuffed tomato, and onion onto skewers. Sprinkle with remaining oil. Place skewers on the grill for 4 - 5 minutes. Optionally, you can add a suitable sauce according to a recipe from this book.

Marinades Recipes

56. Classic Marinade

(Appropriate for meat and fish)

Ingredients:

- 1 large carrot, cut into 8 pieces

- 1 onion, cut into quarters

- 3 - 4 sprigs of parsley coarsely chopped

- 3 - 4 sprigs of fresh thyme

- 1 bay leaf

- ½ teaspoon ground black pepper

- ½ cup sunflower oil or olive oil

- ½ cup wine (white wine - for fish and white meat; red wine for red meat)

Quantity for marinating: 2.25 lb – 3.4 lb (1 kg - 1.5 kg)

Instructions:

Mix all ingredients in a deep pot. Put it on the fire. When the mixture starts to boil, remove the pot and leave it to cool. Then put the meat. If it is for the kebab, it shall be cut into cubes; the fish shall be cleaned from the viscera; the chicken could be whole or cut into portions. When removing the marinade from the meat or fish, leave to drain.

57. Aromatic Marinade for Ribs

(Appropriate for beef ribs and lamb ribs)

Ingredients:

- 2 cloves of garlic, crushed

- 4 - 5 tablespoons soy sauce

- 2 tablespoons honey

- ½ cup wine

- ½ teaspoon ground black pepper

- Pinch of nutmeg

- 2 grains allspice

- 2 cloves

- 1 small cinnamon stick

- 1 tablespoon peel of lemon (or lime), grated

Quantity for marinating: 2.25 lb – 3.4 lb (1 kg - 1.5 kg)

Instructions:

Mix all ingredients in a deep glass bowl. Dip the ribs entirely in the marinade. Put the bowl in the refrigerator for 2 - 3 hours. Then drain the ribs well and put on the grill.

58. Texas Style Marinade

(Appropriate for pork and beef)

Ingredients:

- 1 yellow onion, finely chopped

- 2 tablespoons tomato ketchup

- 4 - 5 tablespoons soy sauce

- 2 tablespoons honey

- 1/3 cup vegetable oil or olive oil

- 2 tablespoons red wine vinegar

- chili pepper sauce to taste

- ½ teaspoon ground black pepper

Quantity for marinating: 2.25 lb – 3.4 lb (1 kg - 1.5 kg)

Instructions:

Put all ingredients in a deep glass bowl. Stir them well. Cover with plastic food wrap and put it in the refrigerator. Use it as quickly as possible after preparation.

59. Garlic Marinade
(Appropriate for beef and lamb)

Ingredients:

- 6 tablespoons sunflower oil

- 2 tablespoons red wine vinegar

- 2 cloves of garlic, crushed

- 2 yellow onions, cut into quarters

- 3 – 4 sprigs fresh thyme

- 1 teaspoon ground black pepper

  Quantity for marinating: 2.25 lb (1 kg)

Instructions:

Put all ingredients in a deep glass bowl. Stir them well. Cover with plastic food wrap and put it in the refrigerator. Meat must stand at least 2 - 3 hours in the marinade. Then drain well and place on the grill.

60. *Special Marinade for Beef*

Ingredients:

- 5 cups cold water

- 1 cup white wine

- ½ cup red wine vinegar

- 1 large fresh carrot, cut into pieces

- 1 yellow onion, cut into pieces

- 2 bay leaves

- 15 - 20 peppercorns

- 2 whole cloves garlic

Quantity for marinating: 2.25 lb – 3.4 lb (1 kg - 1.5 kg)

Instructions:

In a deep pot, mix all the ingredients and cook 30 - 40 minutes.

The meat shall be poured entirely over with the cooled marinade and let stand for 8 - 10 hours in it, upturn it at every

1 - 2 hours. Then the meat can be cook on the grill.

61. Marinade for Chops and Skewers

(Appropriate for chops and skewers)

Ingredients:

- 4 tablespoons vegetable oil or olive oil

- 2 tablespoons soy sauce

- 1 tablespoon brown sugar

- 2 tablespoons balsamic vinegar

- 2 tablespoons dry white wine

- 1 clove garlic, crushed

- ¼ teaspoon ground black pepper

  Quantity for marinating: 2.25 lb (1 kg)

Instructions:

When the meat is brushed with this marinade during the cooking, it becomes glossy and more appetizing.

62. *Japanese Style Marinade*

(Appropriate for pork, beef, and chicken)

Ingredients:

- 4 tablespoons sesame oil
- 4 tablespoons soy sauce
- 6 tablespoons saké
- 2 tablespoons fresh ginger, grated
- 1 clove garlic, crushed
- 1 small sweet onion, finely chopped

  Quantity for marinating: 2.25 lb (1 kg)

Instructions:

The meat shall be mixed with all the products and left to stand in the refrigerator 3 - 4 hours, stirred for every 1 hour. The drained meat place on the grill or BBQ.

63. *Indonesian Style Marinade*

(Appropriate for chicken skewers, lamb)

Ingredients:

- ¼ cup kecap Manis (kecap Manis is a thick, palm sugar-sweetened soy sauce. It's used as a flavoring, marinade or condiment in Indonesian cooking. You can find it in Asian food markets)

- 1 tablespoon peanut or canola oil

- 2 tablespoons soy sauce

- 2 teaspoon ground cumin

- 1 tablespoon rice vinegar

- 1 teaspoon ground coriander

- 3 cloves garlic, crushed

- 1 - 2 teaspoons chili sauce

- ¼ cup smooth natural peanut butter

- 2 tablespoons tomato ketchup

Quantity for marinating: 2.25 lb – 3.4 lb (1 kg - 1.5 kg)

R. Lazarova

Instructions:

The meat shall be mixed with all the products and let stand in the refrigerator (lamb for 6 - 7 hours, chicken for 2 - 3 hours), stirring occasionally. The drained meat place on the grill or BBQ.

64. Marinade for Chicken

Ingredients:

- 2 tablespoons soy sauce

- 2 tablespoons white wine

- 1 - 2 bay leaves

- 2 tablespoons sunflower oil

- ¼ teaspoon ground black pepper

- 1 clove garlic, grated

- juice of ½ lemon

- 1 teaspoon lovage

- 1 tablespoon mustard

Quantity for marinating: 2.25 lb (1 kg)

Instructions:

All ingredients shall be mixed in a deep pot, stir well. Leave in the refrigerator together with the meat for 2 - 3 hours. Drain the meat and cook to grill.

65. Lemon Marinade for Seafood

Ingredients:

- ½ cup olive oil
- a juice of 1 lemon or 1 lime
- peel of 1 lemon or 1 lime, grated
- 1 tablespoon finely chopped parsley
- 2 tablespoons finely chopped dill
- 1 sweet finely chopped onion
- 1 clove garlic, crushed

Quantity for marinating: 2.25 lb (1 kg)

Instructions:

Combine the seafood with all the ingredients. Let marinate in the refrigerator for 15 – 30 minutes, stirring occasionally. The drained seafood place on the grill or BBQ.

66. Citrus Marinade for Turkey, Chicken

Ingredients:

- juice and grated peel of 1 orange

- juice of 1 lime

- 2 cloves garlic, of crushed

- 2 tablespoons sunflower oil

- 1 tablespoon honey or brown sugar

- 2 sprigs fresh rosemary

Quantity for marinating: 2.25 lb – 3.4 lb (1 kg - 1.5 kg)

Instructions:

Combine all the ingredients in a deep bowl. Add the turkey or chicken and stir well. Cover with plastic food wrap and put it in the refrigerator. Meat must stand at least 2 - 3 hours in the marinade. Then drain well and place on the grill.

67. Exotic Marinade for Chicken, Turkey

Ingredients:

- 5 – 6 tablespoon sunflower oil

- juice of 1 lemon

- ½ cup white wine

- 1 teaspoon fresh rosemary

- ¼ teaspoon ground coriander

- ¼ teaspoon spoon nutmegs

- pinch of turmeric powder

- pinch of cinnamon powder

- ½ teaspoon of ground black pepper

Quantity for marinating: 2.25 lb – 3.4 lb (1 kg - 1.5 kg)

Instructions:

Combine chicken (or turkey) with all the ingredients.

Let marinate in the refrigerator for 3 - 4 hours, stirring occasionally. The drained meat and place on the grill or BBQ, during the cooking it shall be sprayed occasionally with marinade.

68. Herb Marinade for Fish

Ingredients:

- 4 tablespoons olive oil

- 1 tablespoon lemon juice

- 3 cloves garlic, finely chopped

- 1 tablespoon finely chopped dill

- a couple of fresh thyme sprigs

- a couple of fresh rosemary sprigs

- ½ teaspoon of ground black pepper

Quantity for marinating: 2.25 lb – 3.4 lb (1 kg - 1.5 kg)

Instructions:

Mix all ingredients in a deep glass bowl. Then cover the fish with marinade. Leave in the refrigerator for about 15 – 30 minutes and place it on the grill.

69. Marinade for Vegetables

Ingredients:

- ¼ cup olive oil or sunflower oil

- juice of ½ lemon

- ½ teaspoon sweet paprika

- ¼ teaspoon ground black pepper

- 1 tablespoon fresh finely chopped cilantro

- 1 tablespoon finely chopped parsley

- 2 sprigs fresh thyme or 2 sprigs fresh rosemary

Quantity for marinating: 2.25 lb – 3.4 lb (1 kg - 1.5 kg)

Instructions:

Combine ingredients and stir well. Grease the vegetables (eggplant, zucchini, carrot, onion, tomato, garlic, and asparagus) with the marinade. Refrigerate for 15 minutes. Place on the grill.

Sauces Recipes

70. Tikka Masala Sauce

(Appropriate for all types of meat, chicken, vegetables)

Ingredients:

- 1 lb (450 g) yellow onion, finely chopped

- 3 clove garlic, crushed

- 1 tablespoon ginger, grated

- 3 tablespoons tomato puree

- 2 tablespoons fresh cream

- 3 tablespoons yogurt

- 3 tablespoons of sunflower oil

- 3 tablespoons lemon juice

- 1 tablespoon honey

- 1 teaspoon sweet paprika

- 1 teaspoon turmeric, ground

- 2 teaspoon cumin, ground

- 2 teaspoon coriander, ground

- 1 teaspoon fennel, ground

- 1 teaspoon cardamom, grounded

- Salt to taste, 1 teaspoon ground black pepper, red chili powder to taste

Instructions:

Blend the ginger and garlic with 2 tablespoons of water in a blender.

Heat the oil in a large frying pan. Add the ground spices and fry then add the onions. Cook the onions gently and slowly until caramelized. Then add a mixture of ginger and garlic and fry gently about 1 - 2 minutes. Add sweet paprika, salt, black pepper, chili powder, tomato puree, and mix well. Finally, add honey, lemon juice, fresh cream, and yogurt and mix well. Add 1/3-cup water if the sauce is too thick.

71. Aioli Sauce

(Appropriate for fish, chicken, vegetables)

Ingredients:

- 1 egg

- 1 egg yolk

- 2 clove garlic, crushed

- 1 tablespoon lemon juice

- 1 tablespoon Dijon mustard

- ½ teaspoon of sea salt

- 1 cup olive oil or sunflower oil

Instructions:

Blend egg, egg yolk, garlic, lemon juice, Dijon mustard, ½-teaspoon sea salt in a blender. Process it at high speed for 2 minutes. Then while the blender is running, pour the olive oil (or sunflower oil) in parts. In about 2 minutes, open the machine. Aioli sauce is ready.

Aioli will keep well in the refrigerator, covered for several days.

72. *Almond Sauce*

(Appropriate for fish, pork, beef and chicken, poultry)

Ingredients:

- 2 oz (55 g) almonds, ground
- 1 clove garlic, crushed
- 4 Roma tomatoes
- 1 tablespoon sweet paprika
- 8 fresh basil leaves
- 7 tablespoons olive oil
- 2 tablespoons apple cider vinegar
- 1 teaspoon brown sugar

Instructions:

Dip the tomatoes for 1 minute in boiling water. Take them out and peel them. With a mixer beat the garlic, tomatoes, brown sugar, and almonds. Add red pepper, basil, and vinegar. To this mixture, add the olive oil to a thin trickle, stirring vigorously.

73. *Sauce with Anchovy Fillets*

(Appropriate for all types of grilled meat, seafood)

Ingredients:

- 4 anchovy fillets, crushed

- 2 tablespoons onion, finely chopped

- 1 clove garlic, crushed

- 2 tablespoons finely chopped parsley

- 7 tablespoons olive oil or sunflower oil

- 2 tablespoons lemon juice

Instructions:

In a glass bowl, combine onion, garlic, anchovy, parsley, and lemon juice. Stir very well. Then add oil in a thin stream, stirring vigorously.

74. Wine Sauce

(Appropriate for beef, turkey)

Ingredients:

- 1 cup red wine

- 1 cup finely chopped yellow onion

- 1 tablespoon butter

- 1 tablespoon flour

- 2 sprig of fresh thyme

- 1 bay leaf

- Ground black pepper to taste, salt to taste

Instructions:

Smother the onion in butter. Add the flour; after 1 minute, add the wine. Stir constantly until the mixture starts to boil. Then put 2/3 cup of cold water, thyme, bay leaf, and black pepper. Allow the mixture to simmer on low heat 10 minutes.

75. Barbecue Sauce

(Appropriate for meat, chicken, sausages, fish)

Ingredients:

- 6 oz can (170 g) tomato paste

- 3 tablespoons olive oil

- 1 tablespoon brandy

- 1 teaspoon Tabasco sauce

- ½ teaspoon curry powder

- 1 teaspoon brown sugar

- 1 tablespoon finely chopped parsley

- 3 – 4 sprigs fresh thyme

- 2 green onions, finely chopped

- 1 tablespoon white onion, finely chopped

Instructions:

In a glass bowl, combine all ingredients and stir vigorously.

76. *Sauce with Dill Pickled Cucumber*

(Appropriate for meat, chicken, turkey)

Ingredients:

- 5 tablespoons olive oil
- 2 yellow onions, finely chopped
- ½ cup dry white wine
- ½ tablespoon apple cider vinegar
- ½ cup of water
- 1 tablespoon Dijon mustard
- 3 dill pickled cucumber, finely chopped
- 1 tablespoon finely chopped parsley
- ¼ teaspoon ground black pepper

Instructions:

In saucepan heat oil of low heat. Add the onions; cook it for 4 -5 minutes. Then add the wine, apple cider vinegar, and water. Sprinkle the mixture with pepper; let it simmer on low heat for 10 minutes. Then back off the mixture from the heat and add the mustard, parsley, and pickled cucumber.

77. Tomato Sauce
(Appropriate for meat, poultry, seafood, cheese, vegetables, mushroom)

Ingredients:

- 3 tablespoons olive oil or sunflower oil

- 1 yellow onion, grated

- 1 fresh medium carrot, grated

- 3 cloves of garlic, crushed

- 1 tablespoon tomato paste

- 1.5 lb (680 g) fresh Roma tomatoes, cut into cubes

- ½ cup white wine

- 1 teaspoon Worcestershire sauce

- 1 teaspoon brown sugar

- ground black pepper to taste, salt to taste

- 1 tablespoon fresh finely chopped oregano or basil

The Indoor Grill Cookbook

Instructions:

In saucepan, heat olive oil or sunflower oil of low heat. Add the onions and carrot, cook for 4 - 5 minutes. Then add the garlic, tomato paste, and tomatoes. After 10 minutes, add the wine, Worcestershire sauce, brown sugar, pepper and salt to taste. When the liquid is evaporated, blend and sprinkle with oregano.

78. Sauce of Roasted Tomatoes

(Appropriate for chicken, fish, vegetables, cheese, mushroom)

Ingredients:

- 2 lb (910 g) fresh Roma tomatoes

- 2 yellow onions

- 3 cloves garlic

- 10 sprigs parsley

- 4 tablespoons olive oil or sunflower oil

- 1 teaspoon brown sugar, ground black pepper to taste, salt to taste

Instructions:

Prick the tomatoes and then roast them for about 3 - 4 minutes on the grill. Then peel tomatoes and put them in a blender for 1 - 2 minutes. Put in a deep bowl; add sugar. Put in blender onion, garlic, olive oil, and parsley for 1 minute. Add them to tomatoes. Season with salt and black pepper; stir well.

79. *English Sauce with Fresh Garden Mint*

(Appropriate for lamb)

Ingredients:

- a large bunch of fresh a common garden mint, leaves

- 5 tablespoons a pure white wine vinegar

- 1 tablespoon brown sugar

- 12 tablespoons boiling water

Instructions:

Pull the leaves from the stalk of the mint. Chop the leaves roughly. Place the chopped mint leaves into a heatproof bowl, sprinkle over the sugar, then pour over the boiling water. Stir gently, cover with cling film, and place to one side and leave to cool. Once cold, add vinegar and stir. Cover again and leave to one side for at least an hour, longer if you have the time. Serve the mint sauce in a small bowl or jug with a small serving spoon. The fresh mint sauce can keep in the refrigerator.

80. *Chimichurri Sauce for Steak*

Ingredients:

- ½ cup olive oil or vegetable oil

- 2 tablespoons red wine vinegar

- 4 tablespoons finely chopped Italian parsley

- 3 cloves garlic, minced

- 1 tablespoon finely chopped chili

- pinch dried oregano

- 4 tablespoons finely chopped Italian parsley

- sea salt to taste, ground black pepper to taste

Instructions:

In a glass bowl, mix all ingredients. Stir well; use the sauce after 10 minutes. Chimichurri Sauce can be prepared, cover, and refrigerated for 1 day before serving.

81. Sauce for Vegetables and Fish

Ingredients:

- 9 oz (250 g) light mayonnaise

- 2 tablespoons tomato ketchup

- 1 clove garlic, crushed

- 1 teaspoon cognac

- ground black pepper to taste

Instructions:

In a glass bowl, mix the ingredients and stir well. Try, if necessary, add salt to taste.

82. *Horseradish Sauce*

(Appropriate for meat, fish, and vegetables)

Ingredients:

- 3 tablespoons prepared horseradish drained

- 2 teaspoons salt

- 1 teaspoon sugar

- ½ cup apple cider vinegar

Instructions:

In a glass bowl, mix all ingredients and mix vigorously. Serve right away. This sauce gives a new taste of grilled meat, fish, and vegetables. Store the sauce in the refrigerator (until 2 weeks).

83. Sour Cream Horseradish Sauce

(Appropriate for beef, poultry)

Ingredients:

- 1 cup sour cream

- 3 tablespoon mayonnaise

- 2 tablespoons prepared horseradish drained

- 1 tablespoon lemon juice

- 1 teaspoon grated lemon peel

- sea salt to taste, ground black pepper to taste

Instructions: Beat the sour cream and mayonnaise. Season with lemon juice, salt, and black pepper, mix well. Add the horseradish and lemon peel, mix again. Serve right away. It may be stored in the refrigerator, covered for 2 – 3 days.

84. Cream Cheese Horseradish Sauce

(Appropriate for vegetables, mushrooms)

Ingredients:

- 8 oz (227 g) cream cheese

- ½ cup natural yogurt

- 2 tablespoons prepared horseradish drained

- 1 clove garlic, grated

- ground black pepper to taste

Instructions:

With an electric mixer on medium, beat the cream cheese, natural yogurt, horseradish, garlic, and black pepper 1 - 2 minutes. (You can refrigerate for up to 2 - 3 days).

85. Buttery Sauce for Fish and Meat

Ingredients:

- 2 tablespoons butter

- 1 tablespoon Dijon mustard

- a juice of 1 lemon

- 1 clove garlic, grated

- ground black pepper to taste

- 1 tablespoon finely chopped Italian parsley

- salt to taste

Instructions:

Melt the butter and add to it the mustard, lemon juice, garlic, and black pepper. Blend the mixture to form a smooth sauce. Finally, add the parsley and salt. Keep the sauce in a warm place, not to curd. It is suitable for pouring hot fish or meat.

86. Tomato Sauce with Mozzarella Cheese

(Appropriate for shrimp, vegetables)

Ingredients:

- 1 yellow onion, finely chopped

- 1.5 lb (680 g) Roma tomatoes, grated

- 3 tablespoons olive oil or sunflower oil

- 3 cloves of garlic, grated

- 15 fresh basil leaves

- 4 tablespoons of grated Mozzarella cheese

- Salt to taste, ground black pepper to taste

Instructions:

Smother the onion and the garlic in the hot oil, and add the tomatoes. Simmer the sauce until it thickens. Remove it from the heat and sprinkle with basil and Mozzarella cheese; then add salt to taste. This sauce can use both hot and cold.

87. Ricotta Cheese Sauce

(Appropriate for vegetables, mushroom)

Ingredients:

- 1 cup Ricotta cheese

- ½ cup natural Greek yogurt

- 2 tablespoons olive oil

- 1 tablespoon lemon juice

- 1 teaspoon curry powder

- 2 tablespoons sliced black olives or green olives

- Herbs of choice (parsley, dill, basil, wild garlic)

- Ground black pepper, salt to taste

Instructions:

In a glass bowl, mix cheese, yogurt, lemon juice, and olive oil. Season it with curry powder, black pepper, and salt to taste. Wash and dry the aromatic herbs thoroughly. Cut them into very small pieces and add them to the mixture. Serve the sauce cooled.

88. Ginger Sauce

(Appropriate for chicken, vegetables)

Ingredients:

- 3 tablespoons apple cider vinegar
- 6 tablespoons sunflower oil
- 2 tablespoons soy sauce
- 2 tablespoons lemon juice
- 2 teaspoons mustard
- 2 tablespoons finely grated ginger
- 2 tablespoons finely chopped onion
- 1 clove garlic, minced
- rosemary to taste, ground black pepper to taste, sea salt to taste

Instructions:

In a glass bowl mix the vinegar, olive oil, lemon juice, and soy sauce, stir well. Then add the mustard, ginger, onion, and garlic. Stir again to obtain a homogeneous mixture.

Season with rosemary, ground black pepper, sea salt.